Always my Daughter... Now my Friend

Celebrating the laughter, joy
and the special bond we share

Inspired
by Faith

Always my Daughter...Now my Friend
ISBN 978-0-9859685-6-4

Published by Product Concept Mfg., Inc.
2175 N. Academy Circle #200, Colorado Springs, CO 80909

©2013 Product Concept Mfg., Inc. All rights reserved.

Written and Compiled by Vicki J. Kuyper
in association with Product Concept Mfg., Inc.

All scripture quotations are from the King James version
of the Bible unless otherwise noted.

Scriptures taken from the Holy Bible,
New International Version®, NIV®.
Copyright © 1973, 1978, 1984 by Biblica, Inc.™
Used by permission of Zondervan.
All rights reserved worldwide.
www.zondervan.com

Sayings not having a credit listed are contributed by writers
for Product Concept Mfg., Inc. or in a rare case,
the author is unknown.

Always my Daughter... Now my Friend

*Memory is the treasury and guardian
of all things.*
Cicero

LIKE MOTHER, LIKE DAUGHTER

When you were small, you used to play dress-up in my heels, whip up an imaginary meal while I hurried to get dinner on the table and mugged in the mirror like a runway model when I put on my make-up. You learned how to walk, talk and tie your shoes by watching, and imitating, me.

But now that you're grown, I watch you with pride–and learn. Whenever I hear someone say to you, "You remind me so much of your mother," I can't help but feel supremely complimented. How I'd love to resemble you in so many wonderful ways.

*A daughter is the happy memories
of the past, the joyful moments
of the present, and the hope and
promise of the future.*

AUTHOR UNKNOWN

*A mother hold's her child's hand
for just a little while—
but she'll be wrapped around
her daughter's pinkie forever!*

It's been said that "mother" is another word for "love." But as any daughter can attest, other synonyms may also include:

Loan officer
Historian
Fashion consultant
Cheerleader
Dressing room valet
On-call babysitter
911 operator
Therapist
Home health care consultant
Legal counsel
    and FRIEND!

IN A MOM'S WORDS...

From the time she could walk and talk my daughter was always marching to her own drumbeat. In an on-going effort to "be a good mom," I continually tried to get her to listen to the music everyone else seemed to hear. If other girls were playing with dolls, she was playing with scissors. If the fashionable color was pink, she chose orange. If she didn't fit in, she'd play alone or find friends who enjoyed scissors and an unconventional wardrobe. It's a miracle we didn't knock each other senseless with all that head-butting. I wanted a "regular" daughter who viewed life like the rest of the crowd.

As my daughter matured, I had a revelation. Many of the girls who'd always followed the crowd seemed rather lost out on their own. Today, my daughter is a beautiful, compassionate, bold young woman. She doesn't let others define her. She's the kind of friend everyone wants…especially me. I've come to value my daughter's unique quirks. I wish every mom could learn this lesson, preferably sooner than I did.

D.K.M.

Let the world know you as you are,
not as you think you should be,
because sooner or later, if you are posing,
you will forget the pose,
and then where will you be?

FANNIE BRICE

A child is not a vase to be filled,
but a fire to be lit.

FRANÇOIS RABELAIS

The greatest happiness in this life
is the conviction we are loved—
loved for ourselves, or rather,
loved in spite of ourselves.
VICTOR HUGO

Risk! Risk anything!
Care no more for the opinions of
others, for those voices. Do the hardest
thing on earth for you.
Act for yourself. Face the truth.
KATHERINE MANSFIELD

The family is like a book—
The children are the leaves,
The parents are the covers
That protecting beauty gives.
At first the pages of the book
Are blank and purely fair,
But Time soon writeth memories
And painteth pictures there.

AUTHOR UNKNOWN

Noteworthy Moms and Daughters

Well-known women's rights activist Elizabeth Cady Stanton often worked from home while caring for her seven children. She was a strategist and theoretician for Susan B. Anthony, a key public speaker for women's suffrage. One of Elizabeth's daughters, Harriot, helped her mother write the *History of Woman Suffrage,* and worked to bring splinter groups of the suffrage movement back together. Harriot's daughter, Nora, was the first American woman to earn a civil engineering degree. She also followed her mother and grandmother's footsteps as an active member of the women's suffrage movement.

In the Words of Elizabeth Cady Stanton...

"Though motherhood is the most important of all the professions—requiring more knowledge than any other department in human affairs—there was no attention given to preparation for this office."

"I would have girls regard themselves not as adjectives but as nouns."

"The heyday of a woman's life is the shady side of fifty."

"Nature never repeats herself, and the possibilities of one human soul will never be found in another."

A daughter is a little girl
who grows up to be a friend.

A picture memory brings to me:
I look across the years and see
Myself beside my mother's knee.
JOHN GREENLEAF WHITTIER

Always I have a chair for you in the
smallest parlor in the world,
to wit, my heart.
EMILY DICKINSON

Epic Failsafe

Let's be honest. The road to friendship for mothers and daughters is bound to hold a few potholes along the way. But when that road gets rough, let's not lose sight of how much we really do love each other…and the fact that mothers hold a treasure trove of potentially embarrassing childhood photos.

Chances are, they've also learned how to use the internet.

So, daughters, do yourself a favor. Keep those lines of communication open between you and your mom. And whatever you do, don't forget Mother's Day!

A Mother's Jewels

Aunt Eleanor wears such diamonds!
   Shiny and gay and grand,
Some on her neck and some in her hair,
   And some on her pretty hand.
One day I asked my mamma
   Why she never wore them, too;
She laughed and said, as she kissed my eyes,
   My jewels are here, bright blue.

"They laugh and dance and beam and smile,
    So lovely all the day,
And never like Aunt Eleanor's go
    In a velvet box to stay.
Hers are prisoned in bands of gold,
    But mine are free as air,
Set in a bonny, dimpled face,
    And shadowed with shining hair!"

Eugene Field

IN A MOM'S WORDS...

When my daughter was just entering her teen years, she and I were headed up a mountain pass for our annual mother/daughter weekend. Though the traffic on our side of the freeway was flowing freely, those headed in the opposite direction were lined up bumper-to-bumper, inching along at a snail's pace for miles. My daughter commented, "Mom, you know that some-where in all those cars is a kid who has to go to the bathroom."

I remember thinking how easily my daughter empathized with those who were younger–that she remembered what it was like to be "just a kid." That's my personal prayer as I get older. I want to try to put myself in my daughter's shoes, recall what it's like to be her age and in her current season in life. I want to take her struggles, her victories, her questions and concerns seriously. I want to empathize, not mini-mize. To simply listen, instead of always jumping in with a "sage" word of advice.

V.J.K

I long to put the experience of fifty years at once into your young lives, to give you at once the key to that treasure chamber every gem of which has cost me tears and struggles and prayers, but you must work for these inward treasures yourselves.

<small>HARRIET BEECHER STOWE</small>

Everyone is the age of their heart.

<small>PROVERB</small>

LESSONS MY MOTHER TAUGHT ME

My mother taught me about...

STAMINA: "You're going to sit there 'til that spinach is finished!"

ARITHMETIC: "If I told you once, I told you a 1,000 times, don't exaggerate!"

ANTICIPATION: "Just wait 'til your father gets home!"

ANATOMY: "Stop crossing your eyes or they'll stay that way!"

LONG-TERM MEMORY: "Where were you born, in a barn?"

LOGIC: "Because I said so, that's why!"

METEOROLOGY: "It looks like a tornado swept through your room!"

JUSTICE: "One" day you'll have kids of your own. Then, you'll understand!"

I always think that in the end the children educate the parents.
PRINCESS ALICE MAUD MARY,
DAUGHTER OF QUEEN VICTORIA

A fluent tongue is the only thing a mother don't like her daughter to resemble her in.
RICHARD BRINSLEY SHERIDAN

The most wasted day of all is that in which we have not laughed.
SÉBASTIEN-ROCH NICOLAS CHAMFORT

God sends us children for another purpose than merely to keep up the race,—to enlarge our hearts, to make us unselfish and full of kindly sympathies and affections; to give our souls higher aims and to call out all of our faculties, to extend enterprise and exertion; to bring round our firesides bright faces and happy smiles, and loving, tender hearts. My soul blesses the great Father every day that He has gladdened the earth with little children.

MARY HOWITT

Of all the joys that lighten suffering earth, what joy is welcomed like a new-born child?

CAROLINE NORTON

*To forget one's ancestors is to be a
brook without a source,
a tree without a root.*

PROVERB

*What is truly indispensable for the
conduct of life has been taught us by
women—the small rules of courtesy,
the actions that win us the warmth
or deference of others; the words
that assure us a welcome;
the attitudes that must be varied
to mesh with character or situation;
all social strategy.*

REMY DE GOURMONT

*In the eyes of its mother every
beetle is a gazelle.*

PROVERB

The angel of the Family is Woman.
Mother, wife, or sister, Woman is
the caress of life, the soothing sweetness
of affection shed over its toils,
a reflection for the individual
of the loving providence which
watches over Humanity. In her there
is treasure enough of consoling
tenderness to allay every pain.

GIUSEPPE MAZZINI

Mom and Daughter Potluck

Not every mother and daughter grow up to become friends. Perhaps it's because the women we wind up with for moms, and for daughters, is kind of like a genetic potluck. We never know who we're going to get. Some mothers who are quiet as church mice give birth to daughters who are natural-born rock stars. Some daughters who love to cook are born to moms who love to eat out. Some moms and daughters struggle just to see eye-to-eye.

But just because moms and daughters are different, doesn't mean they can't grow to become the very closest of friends over time. Even a rocky trip through the teen years doesn't mean that as adults, mothers and daughters can't discover a love for each other that continues to deepen with every passing year. If every mother and daughter is like a covered dish, time allows us to acquire a taste for each other's uniqueness, to savor the sweetness of just spending time together.

IN A DAUGHTER'S WORDS...

Things my Mom used to say...

"You can do anything!"
(She was always my biggest fan.)

"Play outside!"
(Still good advice.)

"CYNTHIA KAY ANDERSON!!!!"
(Never a good thing to hear...)

"I love you so much."
(Always a good thing to hear.)

"I'm so proud of you."
(Always.)

Mom, 10 years ago, a little piece of me went with you. I will forever love and miss you.

C.K.F.

A mother is the truest friend
we have, when trials heavy
and sudden, fall upon us;
when adversity takes the place of
prosperity; when friends who rejoice
with us in our sunshine desert us;
when trouble thickens around us,
still will she cling to us,
and endeavor by her kind precepts
and counsels to dissipate the clouds
of darkness, and cause peace to
return to our hearts.

WASHINGTON IRVING

ALL IN THE FAMILY

A daughter goes to visit her aging mother in the rest home. As she is waiting for her mother to wake up from her afternoon nap, she notices a bowl of peanuts beside her mother's bed and helps herself to one. As time passes, and her mother continues to sleep, the daughter polishes off the entire bowl.

When her mother wakes up, the daughter says apologetically, "Mom! I'm so sorry, but it looks like I finished off all your peanuts."

"That's okay honey," her mother replies. "Without my teeth, all I can do is suck the chocolate off and then spit them back in the bowl anyway."

*My best friend is the one
who brings out the best in me.*

HENRY FORD

*Secret to a happy life:
Treat your friends like family
and your family like friends!*

*Those who bring sunshine
to the lives of others cannot keep
it from themselves.*

J.M. BARRIE

The mother memories that are closest to my heart are the small gentle ones that I have carried over from the days of my childhood. They are not profound, but they have stayed with me through life, and when I am very old, they will still be near…Memories of mother drying my tears, reading aloud, cutting cookies and singing as she did, listening to prayers I said as I knelt with my forehead pressed against her knee, tucking me in bed and turning down the light. They have carried me through the years and given my life such a firm foundation that it does not rock beneath flood or tempest.

MARGARET SANGER

In a Mom's Words...

We started with picture books. My gentle hand guiding your small one over the textures, smooth and rough. As you grew you loved to nestle under my arm while I turned page after page of fanciful rhymes and fairy tales. We cried when things looked bad for the hero and cheered when good won out in the end. We longed to fly on fairy's wings and live in castles in enchanted lands.

As you changed and grew, so did the scope of the books we shared. You learned that not every story ended with "happily every after." But we also read about tenacity, resilience and love. Books have been our touchpoints through the years, our opening to learn about each other, to discover what sparks our dreams, what causes us sorrow, what urges us to act. Even though you're now grown, I hope we always reach together, talk about what we read and seek understanding through words on a page.

C.M.H.

Precepts for the Guidance of a Daughter

(written in 1850)

- Wash your hands.
- **When** you have washed them,
  hold a book in them.
- Diminish your calves.
  Pluck your arms.
- Get up early,
  but not *too* early.
- Talk German so fast
  that no one can ascertain
    whether you speak grammatically
      or not.

- Don't gobble it;
  it turns maidens and turkey-cocks purple.
- Don't swear.
- Assume the power of reading,
  if you have it not.
- Not to leave your room like a hay field,
  of which the grass is gowns and brushes.

Elizabeth Gaskell

Growing Up Together

Over the years, you and I have become teachers to one another. I taught you how to hold a spoon, but you taught me the joy of a ladybug tip-toeing on your finger. I showed you how to walk in heels, but you inspired me to walk tall with a parent's pride as I watched you develop the unique gifts God has given you. You taught me that days turn way too quickly into years—and if I don't slow down and pay attention, I'll miss out on what matters most in life.

You've taught me it's possible to fall in love with someone even before they are born. Not only that, you've taught me that the depth and breadth of a mother's love continues to grow, even once her children are grown.

O young thing,
your mother's lovely armful!
How sweet the fragrance
of your body!
EURIPIDES

It seems a breath of heaven
Round many a cradle lies,
And every little baby
Is a message from the skies.
FRANCES E. W. HARPER

ACROSS THE MILES

All too often, a grown daughter is a distant daughter—in terms of miles, anyway. But that doesn't mean a mother and daughter can't stay close at heart. Here are a couple of ideas to help keep you connected when you live far apart.

- Send wacky postcards from obscure places
- Start a long distance book club
- When she comes to mind, text and let her know.
- On special occasions, text a photo of you celebrating in her honor.
- Hear a song that reminds you of her? Purchase it online and "gift" it to her.
- Call…often.

The world is so empty
if one thinks only
of mountains, rivers and cities;
but to know someone
here and there
who thinks and feels with us,
and though distant,
is close to us in spirit–
this makes the earth for us
an inhabited garden.

JOHANN WOLFGANG VON GOETHE

MOMS AND DAUGHTERS, TAKE NOTE!

Just because we share DNA
doesn't mean we have to share…
   our shoes,
   our cars,
   our PIN numbers,
   our computer passwords,
   the same taste in movies and music,
   our weight,
        OR our dessert!

*The future belongs to those who believe
in the beauty of their dreams.*
ELEANOR ROOSEVELT

*He that would the daughter win
Must with the mother first begin.*
17TH CENTURY PROVERB

*A good laugh
is sunshine in a house.*
WILLIAM MAKEPEACE THACKERAY

NOTEWORTHY MOMS AND DAUGHTERS

Anna Marie Jarvis never knew the joy of becoming a mother, yet she spent her life making certain mothers received the recognition they deserved. After her own mother died, Anna spent her life working to establish a day to honor the contributions mothers make to both family and society.

In 1914, thanks to Anna's diligence, President Woodrow Wilson proclaimed Mother's Day a national holiday. Since Anna's mother's favorite flower was the carnation, it became popular for women to wear a white carnation to honor their mother on that day or a red one if their mother was deceased. However, by 1923, Anna felt that the holiday had become so commercialized that she filed a lawsuit to try to stop it. But Mother's Day prevailed. Today it is celebrated in over 70 countries around the world.

In the Words of Anna Marie Jarvis...

"I want it [Mother's Day] to be a day of sentiment, not profit."

"A printed card means nothing except that you are too lazy to write to the woman who has done more for you than anyone in the world. And candy! You take a box to Mother—and then eat most of it yourself. A pretty sentiment."

"God bless our faithful good mothers."

Mother's Day
Around the World

FRANCE: Until 1945, mothers with four or five children were awarded a bronze medal. Those with six or seven children received a silver medal. Eight or more, a gold!

YUGOSLAVIA: Mother's Day is tied to a 3-week series of holidays, including Children's Day and Father's Day. On Mother's Day the mother is tied up. To earn her freedom she must promise the family candy and baked goods.

FINLAND: On Aidipayiva (Mother's Day) the family gets up early for a walk where they pick flowers which bloom this time of year. They present Mom with the bouquet along with breakfast in bed.

ETHIOPIA: Called Antrosht, this 3-day celebration includes a large family meal. Girls bring butter, cheese, vegetables and spices for the traditional hash recipe, and boys bring a bull or lamb. Mothers and daughters put the butter on their faces and chests. Then the women dance while the men sing songs in honor of family and heroes.

UNITED KINGDOM: The celebration of Mothering Day was prevalent before the American Mother's Day. However, it fell out of practice in the 1900s. After WWII, Great Britain picked up the American tradition. On this day, Moms receive cakes and flowers (usually violets). It's customary to serve Simnel Cake—a glazed fruitcake inspired by a folk tale about a married couple, Simon and Nell. Supposedly, the pair could not decide whether to bake or broil a cake, so they did both—and the Simnel Cake was born.

Mother's love grows by giving.

CHARLES LAMB

A mother's heart
is always with her children.

PROVERB

Most of all the other beautiful things
in life come by twos and threes by
dozens and hundreds. Plenty of roses,
stars, sunsets, rainbows, brothers, and
sisters, aunts and cousins, but only one
mother in the whole world.

KATE DOUGLAS WIGGIN

"Maternal love,"
like an orange tree, buds and blossoms
and bears at once. When a true woman
puts her finger for the first time into
the tiny hand of her baby and feels that
helpless clutch which tightens her very
heartstrings, she is born again with
the newborn child.

KATE DOUGLAS WIGGIN

Thou art thy mother's glass,
and she in thee
Calls back the lovely April of
her prime.

WILLIAM SHAKESPEARE

Mom's Magnetic Personality

An elementary teacher was preparing to discuss magnetism with her class. She held a magnet over a box filled with pins and then said, "My name begins with m and I pick up things. What am I?"

A girl in the front row immediately yelled out, "MOM!"

*Our daughters are the most precious
of our treasures, the dearest possessions
of our homes and the objects of
our most watchful love.*

MARGARET E. SANGSTER

*The mother should teach her daughter
above all things to know herself.*

C.E. SARGENT

*A daughter is a treasure—
and a cause of sleeplessness.*

BEN SIRACH

IN A MOM'S WORDS...

My daughter and I moved to South Africa when she was 11. Until then she'd never written an exam at school. She joined a new school at the end of the year, during final exams–about stuff she hadn't learned yet! Rather daunting. In order to soften the blow, I decided to write words of encouragement for every exam. I wrote them on napkins, which I snuck into her lunchbox along with a snack.

The tradition stuck. Over the years my daughter shared how she derived encouragement, laughter, gratitude and sometimes tears of joy from the loving well wishes laced with off-beat humor. My daughter, now 18, wrote her final high school exam this past week. How much I'll miss our "napkin love." Though those tough exams may be over, the memories of the smiles we shared over those simple words of encouragement will remain in our hearts for life.

G.K.

A Bit of "Napkin Love"

Dear Chickpea,

Today is your biology exam;
You would have preferred grilled cheese with ham…
Just do you best; don't fret the rest
You're a star, no matter what—
Good luck, Ma'am!

Love you lots and lots, MOMMY
XOXOXOX

*Oh my son's my son till he
gets him a wife, but my daughter's
my daughter all her life.*

DINAH MARIA MULOCK CRAIK

*For a wife,
take the daughter of a good mother.*

THOMAS FULLER

*What a grand thing, to be loved!
What a grander thing still, to love!*

VICTOR HUGO

OPEN LETTER TO DAUGHTERS EVERYWHERE

Daughters, please take note: We don't want to push you. (Well, maybe we do want to give you a little nudge in the right direction!) But we really would appreciate it if you'd get married. It's not that we are desperate for grandkids. (Okay, so maybe that's a half-truth. We really would like grandkids, as long as that doesn't make us "grandmothers," because frankly that sounds way too old and wrinkly.)

What we REALLY want is a chance to dress up. An opportunity like that presents itself so rarely these days. But your wedding (and the bridal shower and rehearsal dinner that precede it) would give us the chance to shop for something lovely and flouncey. Something that would make us feel young and beautiful. Even if just for a few hours. Of course, we do want you to be happy. So, take your time and get engaged to an absolutely fantastic guy who loves you more than life itself. But if at all possible, please keep that engagement short. Think of your mother!

P.S. And whatever you do, don't elope!

It isn't so much what's on the table
that matters, as what's on the chairs.

W.S. GILBERT

If children grew up according to early
indication, we should have nothing but
geniuses.

JOHANN WOLFGANG VON GOETHE

A mom should always keep
her mind open, her heart soft
and her cookie jar full.

OUTSIDE THE SPOTLIGHT

Most mothers and daughters never win a Nobel Prize or Academy Award, write a bestselling novel or grace the cover of a magazine. But that doesn't mean they aren't smart, talented, beautiful or significant. It simply means they share their unique gifts with a smaller audience—that of family and friends.

Consider your own mom. What award has she earned in your eyes? Has she gone "Above and Beyond" in understanding? Does her "Love and Loyalty" never seem to run dry? Is she a "Friend Extraordinaire" who's always ready to listen or lend a hand when you need her most?

Here's to all the moms and daughters who live–and love–outside the spotlight. May they never forget how amazing they really are!

You May Have Become Your Mother, If...

...You do a double-take every time you pass a mirror.

...You defend "mom jeans" as a viable fashion choice.

...You fall asleep before the ball drops on New Year's Eve.

...You remember your cholesterol levels but forget your age.

...You hear yourself proclaim, "Because I said so!"

...You see your mother in a photo– and then realize she's wearing your clothes.

Give me a sense of humor, Lord,
Give me the grace to see a joke;
To get some happiness from life,
And pass it on to other folk.

PRAYER FROM CHESTER CATHEDRAL, UK

I'm not saying she was very silly,
but one of us was very silly
and it wasn't me.

ELIZABETH GASKELL

As long as a woman can look ten
years younger than her daughter she is
perfectly satisfied.

OSCAR WILDE

Noteworthy Moms and Daughters (In-Law!)

Anna Mary Robertson was a farm girl with a limited education when she married Thomas Salmon Moses. They had 10 children, five of whom died at birth. Besides working the farm, Anna enjoyed needlework, sewing and embroidery. But in her late 70s, Anna took up painting, because it was easier on her arthritic hands.

A few of Anna's paintings were on display in a drugstore window when a visiting art collector noticed them. Anna's daughter-in-law told the collector that "Grandma Moses" had ten more paintings she might sell. It turned out Anna only had nine paintings. So Anna cut a large painting in half and reframed it. Artwork Anna once sold for $5 was soon selling for $8,000 to $10,000. At the age of 100, Grandma Moses illustrated *Twas the Night Before Christmas.* She died at the age of 101.

In the Words of Grandma Moses...

"If people want to make a fuss over me,
I let 'em, but I was the same person before
as I am now."

"Life is what we make it. Always has
been, always will be."

"If I hadn't started painting, I would
have raised chickens."

"I have written my life in small sketches,
a little today, a little yesterday…I look
back on my life a good day's work, it was
done and I feel satisfied with it. I made
the best out of what life offered."

It is as grandmothers that our mothers come into the fullness of their grace.

CHRISTOPHER MORLEY

Being pretty on the inside means you don't hit your brother and you eat all your peas– that's what my grandma taught me.

LORD CHESTERFIELD

A house needs a grandma in it.

LOUISA MAY ALCOTT

In a (Grand)Daughter's Words...

Grandmothers, mothers, daughters, granddaughters...we're all part of a conga line of wonderful women born into the same family, who've been given the opportunity to also grow into the closest of friends. My grandmother was like a second Mom. She was such a dear friend I asked her to be a bridesmaid in my wedding. I promised I'd find a cute young guy to accompany her down the aisle. She declined with a laugh, saying she was too old to parade around in a fancy dress in front of so many people. Even though she sat on the sidelines on my wedding day, my grandmother knew she was just as important—if not more—than my closest friends who stood by my side.

My grandmother died over twenty years ago. But just last night I dreamed we were on a cruise ship together, laughing and chatting and enjoying the azure blue of the sea. Nothing can separate us from the love of those who've first loved us.

V.J.K.

*If becoming a grandmother
was only a matter of choice,
I should advise every one of you
straight away to become one. There is
no fun for old people like it!*

HANNAH WHITALL SMITH

*Grandmas are moms
with lots of frosting.*

ANONYMOUS GRANDKID

*By the time the youngest children
have learned to keep the house tidy,
the oldest grandchildren are
on hand to tear it to pieces.*

CHRISTOPHER MORLEY

A grandmother is a babysitter who watches kids instead of the television.

*Children's children
are a crown to the aged,
and parents are the pride
of their children.*
PROVERBS 17:6 NIV

*Truly there is nothing
in the world so blessed or
so sweet as the heritage of children.*
MARGARET OLIPHANT

*Grandkids fill a space in your heart you
never realized was empty.*

To My Daughter

Just being in your company
makes me believe I'm on vacation.
You turn even the smallest joy
into full-blown celebration.
You act as though loving others well
is your personal vocation.
You're more than just a daughter to me—
You're my favorite inspiration!

VICKI J. KUYPER

*I bring my children up
as simply and with as few wants
as I can, and above all, teach them
to help themselves and others,
so as to become independent.*

PRINCESS ALICE MAUD MARY,
DAUGHTER OF QUEEN VICTORIA

*And thou shalt in thy daughter see,
This picture, once, resembled thee.*

AMBROSE PHILIPS

*There's only one pretty child in the
world and every mother has it.*

PROVERB

NOTEWORTHY MOMS AND DAUGHTERS

Mary Wollstonecraft was a 19th century British writer, philosopher and advocate of women's rights whose first publication was entitled, *Thoughts on the Education of Daughters*. Unfortunately, Mary died shortly after the birth of her second daughter, also named Mary. Nonetheless, this daughter followed in her mother's footsteps and also became a well-known author.

Mary Wollstonecraft Shelley's first novel was inspired by a dream and written in response to a bet with her husband. It was titled, *Frankenstein*. At the time, many people believed Mary's husband, the renowned poet Percy Bysshe Shelley, must have written the story, because they questioned whether a 19-year-old girl could possibly pen such a scary story. More than 50 films have been made based on Mary's novel. Upon her death, Mary Shelley asked to be buried with her mother.

*Strengthen the female mind
by enlarging it.*
MARY WOLLSTONECRAFT

*Surely something resides
in the heart that is not perishable—
and life is more than a dream.*
MARY WOLLSTONECRAFT

*It is hardly surprising that
women concentrate on the way they
look instead of what is in their minds
since not much has been put in their
minds to begin with.*
MARY WOLLSTONECRAFT SHELLEY

*This little girl, our darling, is become a
most intelligent little creature,
and as gay as a lark, and that in the
morning, too, which I do not find
quite so convenient.*
MARY WOLLSTONECRAFT SHELLEY

To Each Her Own Life

Sometimes, having a daughter feels like a second chance…To go to the prom. To be beautiful. To get chosen for the team. To make our mark on the world. To watch our dreams come true. But make no mistake, you and I are individuals. You are your own uniquely gifted woman with your own life stories to write, with your own successes… and failures.

Living vicariously through you wouldn't do justice to anyone. It's fantasy, not reality. It keep us, as moms, from fully experiencing today through our own eyes. And it diminishes the significance, and singular journey, of the amazing women we have the privilege of calling "daughter."

Daughters need breathing room to live their own lives and become the women they were born to be. The same is true for moms. Just like half-baked brownies, neither of us are done yet!

We have no power
   to fashion our children as suits our will;
As they are given by God,
   so we must have them and love them;
Teach them as best we can,
   and let each of them follow his nature.
One will have talents of one sort,
   and different talents another.
Every one uses his own:
   each must be happy and good.

JOHANN WOLFGANG VON GOETHE

In a Mom's Words...

I'm not a crier. So, I never considered my own tears would make an appearance at my daughter's wedding. But right after my husband walked our beautiful daughter down the aisle, we took part in the "give your daughter away" ritual. I hugged my soon-to-be son-in-law, welcoming him to our family. Then, I embraced my daughter... and the tears started to flow. The only word I could choke out was, "Good-bye."

It was so unexpected, that I didn't understand until later why I'd reacted that way. My daughter had previously married a man who had no control over his anger. I never fully trusted him with her heart. Today—for the first time—I really was "giving my daughter away." I was placing her in the care of a man who I wholeheartedly trusted to love her well. Seeing your daughter get married is like letting go of one treasure so you can freely grab hold of a totally different one. All I can say is my daughter's relationship with her husband continues to bring tears to my eyes...for all the right reasons.

V.J.K.

On your daughter's wedding day
There's something you should know:
It's the height of multi-tasking—
Holding on and letting go.

There is no more lovely, friendly and
charming relationship, communion or
company than a good marriage.
MARTIN LUTHER

Happy is the man who finds a true
friend, and far happier is he who finds
that true friend in his wife.
FRANZ SCHUBERT

THE FACTS OF LIFE

The minute little Janey got home from school she excitedly told her mother, "Today in class we learned how to make babies!"

Trying to keep her cool, her mother responded, "That's interesting, honey. How do you do that?"

Janey said confidently, "Change the 'y' to 'i' and add 'es.'"

If I were to choose among all the gifts
and qualities that which, on the whole,
makes life pleasantest,
I should select the love of children.

THOMAS HIGGINSON

A perplexing and ticklish
possession is a daughter.

THOMAS HARDY

Oh, the comfort—
the inexpressible comfort of
feeling safe with a person—
having neither to weigh thoughts
nor measure words,
but pouring them all right out,
just as they are,
chaff and grain together,
certain that a faithful hand
will take and sift them,
keep what is worth keeping,
and then with a breath of
kindness blow the rest away.

DINAH MARIA MULOCK CRAIK

THE CARE AND FEEDING OF A FRIEND'S HEART

Friendship between moms and daughters is an amazing gift. It's also a tricky one. After all, we both know way too much about each other. We've seen each other at our best and at our worst. We feel so comfortable in one another's company that we're liable to say anything at any time–often before thinking it through. If we're not careful, we may find ourselves taking each other for granted in ways we would never dream of doing with the other women in our circle of friends.

With so many shared memories, we may feel as though we know each other inside and out. But there's always more to discover about those we love. Let's explore!

Ask questions. Really listen. Expect the unexpected! Most of all, let's treat one another with the same courtesy, respect, commitment and candor as we do our dearest friends. After all, moms and daughters are more than just chance acquaintances. We're linked by love for a lifetime.

F. Scott Fitzgerald's Advice to His Daughter...

Things to worry about:
Worry about courage
Worry about cleanliness
Worry about efficiency
Worry about horsemanship...

Things not to worry about:
Don't worry about popular opinion
Don't worry about dolls
Don't worry about the past

Don't worry about the future
Don't worry about growing up
Don't worry about anybody
  getting ahead of you
Don't worry about triumph
Don't worry about failure
  unless it comes through your own fault…

The first great gift we can bestow on
others is a good example.

THOMAS MORELL

Maternal love!
Thou word that sums all bliss.

ROBERT POLLOK

It is impossible to estimate
too highly the value and the
helpfulness of a true home of love.
Home is a shelter. Young lives nest there
and find warmth and protection.

J. R. MILLER

These are my Jewels

Cornelia, the mother of the Gracchi, once entertained a woman from Campania at her house. Since the woman made a great show of her jewels, which were among the most beautiful of the time, Cornelia detained her in conversation until her children came home from school. Then, pointing to her children, she said, "These are my jewels."

VALERIUS MAXIMUS, 1ST CENTURY

*Home is where the great
are small and the small are great.*

ANONYMOUS

*Every baby born into the world
is a finer one than the last.*

CHARLES DICKENS

*Friendship is a strong and habitual
inclination in two persons to promote
the good and happiness of one another.*

EUSTACE BUDGELL

In a Mom's Words...

Once upon a time, my daughter was born! I memorized her perfect face and the feel of her soft, silky skin, wanting this season to last forever, yet knowing the bittersweet reality. Even at a young age, she showed great patience and grace, allowing me to dress her up like a human baby doll.

Watching her grow into such a beautiful young lady has been an exceptional honor. She's faced adversity, yet remained strong, despite my great weakness. It was my job as her mother to protect her and guide her, but together we learned to turn to God for those things no human could provide. I hold such admiration for my daughter's strength, courage, wisdom and drive. Her heart and faith is what I strive for. I thought it was my role as her mother to teach her the way to go. Now I believe she was sent here to teach me. My daughter is my greatest hero. When I grow up I want to be just like her!

L.M.B.

THE DAY YOU WERE BORN...

Only a baby small,
        Dropt from the skies;
Only a laughing face,
        Two sunny eyes.
Only two cherry lips,
        One chubby nose,
Only two little hands,
        Ten little toes.

Only a tender flower,
    Sent us to rear.
Only a life to love,
    While we are here.
Only a baby small,
    Never at rest,
Small, but how dear to us,
    God knoweth best.

MATTHIAS BARR

Noteworthy Moms and Daughters

The word "noteworthy" doesn't do justice to the Curie family. They have the distinction of having more Nobel laureates than any other family. Not only was Marie Curie the first woman to win a Nobel Prize, she's also one of only four people to win twice (for Physics and Chemistry).

In 1906, Marie's Nobel laureate husband, Pierre, was killed in a horse carriage accident, leaving Marie to raise their two small daughters. As a single mother, Madame Curie became the first woman professor at the Sorbonne in Paris. In 1935, Marie's eldest daughter, Irène Joliot-Curie won a Nobel Prize (along with her husband) in Chemistry. Marie's younger daughter, Ève, wrote a biography of her mother that later became a motion picture.

Nothing in life is to be feared.
It is only to be understood.

MARIE CURIE

That one must do some work
seriously and must be independent
and not merely amuse oneself in life—
this our mother has told us always,
but never that science was the only
career worth following.

IRÈNE JOLIOT-CURIE

One never notices what
has been done; one can only see
what remains to be done.

MARIE CURIE

We never know the love of the parent
till we become parents ourselves.

HENRY WARD BEECHER

To everything there is a season,
and a time to every purpose under the
heaven…a time to weep,
and a time to laugh; a time to mourn,
and a time to dance.

ECCLESIASTES 3:1, 4

Light tomorrow with today.

ELIZABETH BARRETT BROWNING

THE STAGES OF MOTHERHOOD
(FROM A DAUGHTER'S POINT OF VIEW)

4 YEARS OLD:
My Mommy can do anything!

8 YEARS OLD:
My Mom knows a lot! A whole lot!

12 YEARS OLD:
I guess Mom doesn't know everything.

14 YEARS OLD:
Nope, she doesn't know that either…

16 YEARS OLD:
Mom? She's hopeless!

18 YEARS OLD:
MY mother? She's soooo out of touch!

25 YEARS OLD:
Mom might know something about that…

35 YEARS OLD:
Before we decide, let's get Mom's opinion.

65 YEARS OLD:
Wish I could talk it over with Mom…

Motherly Advice From Eleanor Roosevelt

"No one can make you feel inferior without your consent."

"A woman is like a tea bag; you never know how strong it is until it's in hot water."

"Do what you feel in your heart to be right— for you'll be criticized anyway."

"You wouldn't worry so much about what others think of you if you realized how seldom they do."

"Learn from the mistakes of others. You can't live long enough to make them all yourself."

"It is not fair to ask of others what you are not willing to do yourself."

"Do one thing every day that scares you."

"You can often change your circumstances by changing your attitude."

"Beautiful young people are accidents of nature, but beautiful old people are works of art."

Daughter =
Fountain of Youth

Having a grown daughter keeps a mother young. After all, it's you who tell us our jeans are too high and our driving is too slow. You help update our slang, our shoes and our tastebuds. Who knew we should be eating cake pops instead of cupcakes, beignets instead of doughnuts and kale chips instead of French fries? You've opened our eyes to gluten-free, vegan, organic and dining at food trucks. Where would we be without you?

Yes, without you we'd continue to hum in the grocery store, convinced they've improved their musical selection–when the truth is the sound track of our generation has been demoted to elevator music. Thank goodness you've introduced us to contemporary stations, with words we can't understand and a beat we can't dance to. Thanks to you we no longer look or act old. We're simply more aware of how old we really are.

You know you're getting older,
when you choose your cereal
for the fiber, instead of the toy.

Life would be infinitely happier if we
could only be born at the age of eighty
and gradually approach eighteen.
MARK TWAIN

Age is just a number.
Mine will remain unlisted.

When grace is joined with wrinkles,
it is adorable.
VICTOR HUGO

YOUR MOTHER'S PRAYER

It's me again, God,
    with the same old prayer…
For the wonderful daughter
    You've placed in my care.
Remind her to floss
    and to eat her greens,
To fasten her seatbelt
    and keep her room clean,
To date only nice guys,
    be modest in dress,
To speak only kind words—
    even with PMS.
For You know she'll always
    be my little girl,
The smartest and prettiest found
    in the whole world!
Thank you for sending me
    such a sweet friend,
In the gift of a daughter—
    what a blessing! Amen.

In a Mom's Words...

My daughter has helped build water systems in the Dominican Republic, dig latrines in Honduras, construct homes in Mexico, supervise children in foster care and counsel emotionally disturbed teens. She's been up-close-and-personal with poverty, tragedy, mental illness, abuse and neglect. And she's not even thirty yet.

The word "proud" isn't broad enough to describe how I feel about my daughter. And as every mom knows, even the word "love" seems so slight in light of how deeply I feel connected to her. Do I worry about the weight she carries? I wouldn't be a mom, if I didn't. But when I hear people bemoan the younger generation and the condition of the world, I can't help but think about my daughter and her circle of friends— and rest assured that the future is in capable, compassionate hands.

V.J.K.

NOTEWORTHY MOMS AND DAUGHTERS

It's true that the relationship between Marmee and her four daughters (Meg, Jo, Beth and Amy) was conceived in Louisa May Alcott's imagination and given birth through her novel *Little Women*. But that doesn't mean that this fictional relationship isn't noteworthy–or that it doesn't continue to live on in the hearts of generation after generation of mothers and daughters. In an era when women were rarely urged to follow their own dreams, Marmee helped each of her daughters discover their own unique beauty and gifts–and encouraged them to live lives that were in line with who they were created to be. That's a mother who's also a friend!

Little Women was inspired by Louisa May Alcott's relationship with her own three sisters, Abigail, Elizabeth and Anna, and her mother, Abigail. Louisa's writing helped support her family through some extremely lean years.

In the Words of
Louisa May Alcott

*"What do girls do who haven't any mothers
to help them through their troubles?"*

*"The clocks were striking midnight and the
rooms were very still as a figure glided quietly
from bed to bed, smoothing a coverlid here,
settling a pillow there, and pausing to look
long and tenderly at each unconscious face,
to kiss each with lips that mutely blessed,
and to pray the fervent prayers which only
mothers utter."*

*"Mothers can forgive anything! Tell me
all, and be sure that I will never let you go,
though the whole world should turn
from you."*

*"She rejoiced as only mothers can in the
good fortunes of their children."*

In a Mom's Words...

A wise man once advised me, "Read, read, read, and don't worry so much what other people think of you." My dear daughter, as you make your own life away from our family home, I pass this advice to you: Read newspapers, magazines, food labels, warnings and the fine print. Read graffiti, scribbles on bathroom stalls and poetry. Most of all read books. Fiction, nonfiction, weighty tomes, fluffy romances, graphic novels, history, fantasy, mystery, thriller, religious works–read it all. Then talk about what you read with loved ones, colleagues at work and strangers in the grocery store.

The whole of the human experience can be found in books. Read them to discover and understand yourself and those around you. Read them to be awed by the sacred and the unknowable wonders of the world. And don't forget to read sometimes just for fun.

C.M.H.

There are books which take rank
in our life with parents and lovers
and passionate experiences.

RALPH WALDO EMERSON

Books are the food of youth,
the delight of old age.

CICERO

If your daughters are inclined
to love reading, do not check their
inclination by hindering them of the
diverting part of it. It is as necessary
for the amusement of women
as the reputation of men.

MARY WORTLEY MONTAGU

MOTHERLY ADVICE

When your mother asks, "Do you want my advice?" it's a mere formality. Brace yourself, because that advice is coming your way, regardless of your answer! Here's just a sample of what you can expect:

"If God had wanted you to have holes in your eyebrows He would have put them there!"

"You will eat that and you will LIKE it!"

"The best way to get a man to do something is to suggest he's too old for it!"

"You'll break your arm patting yourself on the back!"

"Don't put that in your mouth; you don't know where it's been!"

"What do you do when your boyfriend walks out? Shut the door!"

*I sometimes give myself admirable
advice, but I am incapable of taking it.*

MARY WORTLEY MONTAGU

*A mother's children are like ideas;
none are as wonderful as her own.*

PROVERB

*See to it that your boys and girls, when
they grow up, do not remember you as
an anxious, worried, irritable mother;
but live such a trustful life before them
that they will have always a picture of
peace and trust when they think of you.*

HANNAH WHITALL SMITH

I Am A Mom

The men of influence, the movers
and shakers, people of power…

My power lies in always having a
tissue tucked somewhere in my purse
for a runny nose.

It can be felt in my big hand that safely
holds a little one through a parking lot.

My strength is in my soft side when
my arm draws a child in close to listen
to a story.

The world trembles at my mighty
influence when I teach a child how
our words go out once and never
come back.

Even in silence, I wield force as I listen,
Moment by moment, year by year
  to the stories
  and the dreams
  and the hurts
  and the worries
  and the joys
  and the fears
  and the questions
Of those hearts for which I bear
  responsibility to love.
I am easy to take for granted.
But I am impossible to overestimate.

KIMBERLEY U. SCOTT

In conversation father can
Do many wondrous things;
He's built upon a wiser plan
Than presidents or kings.
He knows the ins and outs of each
And every deep transaction;
We look to him for theories,
But look to ma for action.

EDGAR A. GUEST

He wields a mighty sceptre,
O'er lesser powers that be,
But a mightier power and stronger,
Man from his throne has hurled,
And the hand that rocks the cradle,
Is the hand that rules the world.

WILLIAM ROSS WALLACE

Who can find a virtuous woman?
for her price is far above rubies…
Her children arise up, and call
her blessed; Her husband also, and he
praiseth her. Many daughters
have done virtuously, but thou
excellest them all.

<small>PROVERBS 31:10, 28–29</small>

A happy family
is but an earlier heaven.

<small>SIR JOHN BOWRING</small>

If you make children happy now,
you will make them happy twenty
years hence by the memory of it.

<small>SYDNEY SMITH</small>

In a Daughter's Words...

When I was in elementary school, my sister and I decided we were mature enough to live on our own. At least for one night. So we told our mother we were "running away." Then we lugged our sleeping bags, pillows, PB & J sandwiches and a box of cereal out to our backyard fort to spend the night. We awoke at dawn to a damp, gray blanket of fog that had settled over the coastal area where we lived. As we ate our cold cereal, wrapped tightly in our sleeping bags, we saw something being lowered by a rope off the back balcony of our house. It was a thermos filled with hot chocolate, courtesy of Mom.

Today, as a grown woman, I still "pretend" to be self-sufficient. But every so often, my mom sends me an unexpected gift, a check, a word of encouragement or a piece of much-needed advice. In her own way, my mom is still offering me a cup of cocoa when I need it most.

V.J.K.

*Women know
The way to rear up children (to be just).
They know a simple, merry, tender knack
of tying sashes, fitting baby-shoes
and stringing pretty words that make no sense.*

ELIZABETH BARRETT BROWNING

Women are the real architects of society.

HARRIET BEECHER STOWE

I love these little people;
and it is not a slight thing when they,
who are so fresh from God, love us.
CHARLES DICKENS

I thank my God upon
every remembrance of you.
PHILIPPIANS 1:3

A mother's prayers, silent and gentle,
can never miss the road to
the throne of all bounty.
HENRY WARD BEECHER

You will find as you look back upon your life that the moments when you have truly lived are the moments when you have done things in the spirit of love.

HENRY DRUMMOND

Beauty is expression. When I paint a mother I try to render her beautiful by the mere look she gives her child.

JEAN-FRANÇOIS MILLET

When God thought of Mother, He must have laughed with satisfactions— so rich, so deep, so full of power and beauty was the conception.

HENRY WARD BEECHER

*A child's soul is more tender
and vulnerable than the finest or
tenderest plant, and a cross look or a
rough touch or an unkind tone is often
sufficient to inflict a savage blow. God
grant that every mother may recognize
in time the sacredness and tenderness
of the soul of her child!*

HANNAH WHITALL SMITH

*Oh, what a power is motherhood,
possessing a potent spell.
All women alike.
Fight fiercely for a child.*

EURIPEDES

Sweater, n.: garment worn by child
when its mother is feeling chilly.

AMBROSE BIERCE

Happiness is not a goal…
it's a by-product of a life well lived.

ELEANOR ROOSEVELT

Oh, the love of a mother,
love which none can forget.

VICTOR HUGO

I loved you enough…
…to say "no."
…to make sure you ate your vegetables.
…to set a curfew.
…to not buy you everything you wanted.
…to allow you to fail.
…to refuse to allow you to measure your worth
   by the number on a scale.
…to be a mom when you were little,
   instead of your best friend,
   so I can be a friend to you now that you're grown—
   one who's so proud to also be your Mom.

In a Mom's Words...

My daughter Kalena truly is my best friend. When I say that, I mean she's the best example of a beautiful, godly woman in my life. She's the kind of woman I aspire to be. She's smart, beautiful, warm, loving, a good wife and so giving. I know that having raised such a great person is one of my greatest accomplishments. When I need to tell someone anything–something funny I saw, a frustration, or something I did that I am proud of–Kalena is the first person I want to tell.

My daughter's full name is Jasmine Kalenaleilani. It means "my beautiful gift from God." She truly has been that gift to me and I thank God for her every day.

K.M.C.

Mothers see the angel
in us because the angel is there.

BOOTH TARKINGTON

I never thought that you
should be rewarded for the
greatest privilege of life."

MARY ROPER COKER,
MOTHER OF THE YEAR IN 1958

*When the heart overflows with
gratitude or with any other sweet
and sacred sentiment, what is the word
to which it would give utterance?
A friend.*

WALTER SAVAGE LANDOR

*A mother's arms are made
of tenderness and children sleep
soundly in them.*

VICTOR HUGO

*Every human being is intended
to have a character of his own;
to be what no others are,
and to do what no other can.*

WILLIAM ELLERY CHANNING

*Of all the blessings
that we receive,
—big or small—
that heaven sends,
what could compare
with a blessing as rare
as giving birth
to your very best friend?*

A friend loveth at all times.

PROVERBS 17:17

May God grant you always…
A sunbeam to warm you,
A moonbeam to charm you,
A sheltering Angel so nothing can harm you.
Laughter to cheer you.
Faithful friends near you.
And when you pray,
For Heaven to hear you.

BLESSING

A Flower for Thought

A young woman stopped at a flower shop to wire flowers to her mother who lived a few hours away. She noticed a little girl on the curb outside the shop, crying, so she asked her what was wrong. "I wanted to get my mother a rose for Mother's Day, but they cost one dollar and I only have seventy-five cents."

The young woman smiled. "Don't worry," she said. "I'll help you pay for the rose." So, she did. After ordering her own mother's bouquet to be delivered, the young woman offered to walk the girl home. The little girl replied, "I'm not headed home yet, but could you come with me to give my mother her flower?"

"I'd be delighted to," said the young woman. The little girl led the woman to a nearby cemetery, where she placed the flower on a freshly dug grave. Shortly afterward, the young woman returned to the flower shop, cancelled her order, purchased a fresh bouquet and drove to her mother's house to deliver them in person.

Think naught a trifle,
though it small appear;
Small sands the mountain,
moments make the year,
And trifles life.

EDWARD YOUNG

Time is a very precious gift of God;
so precious that it's only given
to us moment by moment.

AMELIA BARR

So teach us to number
our days, that we may apply
our hearts unto wisdom.

PSALM 90:12

The Myth of the Perfect Mom

There have undoubtedly been times I've failed you as a mother, days when my words were sharp and my heart, hard. I could blame it on hormones, a lack of sleep or caffeine…or that fact that moms have hard days, too. But if I'm honest with myself–and you– I know the heart of the problem was that I lost sight of the blessing it is to be your mom.

Sure, raising any child is going to have its share of struggles and heartache. But, being able to call you "daughter" is, and always will be, one of the greatest privileges I've ever received. Forgive me for the times I've offered less than the best I had to give. As you grew, so did I. I'm still learning.

One thing I never had to learn was how to love you. You taught me to believe in love at first sight.

My daughter, you're so gifted;
there's so much that you can do!
I've come to learn some wondrous things
by simply watching you.
But I have one request
I think may be long overdue:
You know I pray for you each day...
Would you pray for me, too?

In a Mom's Words...

As a foster and adoptive mom, building courage and trust into the children who pass through my life has been my goal. My daughter came through the door believing she was ugly and stupid. That's what the adults in her life had told her. She had endured much neglect and abuse in her early days; it was hard for her to believe anything an adult could say. I could see the hurt and mistrust in her eyes. From where she came from, I was just another adult coming in to hurt her.

Many visits and interactions slowly began to build into a friendship. She trusted me. Over the years, I saw those frightened eyes melt into gateways to her soul. Now she can finally see how smart and beautiful she really is. She's taught me about being real, honest and God-trusting. Her coming to me was a gift from God. He answered my heart's desire and I'm blessed to be a mom of a daughter who's also a friend!

T.M.L.

The beggarly question of parentage—
what is it, after all?
What does it matter, when you
come to think of it, whether a child
is yours by blood or not?
THOMAS HARDY

Give a little love to a child,
and you get a great deal back.
JOHN RUSKIN

Encouragement is oxygen to the soul.
GEORGE M. ADAMS

They talk about a woman's sphere as
though it had a limit;
There's not a place in earth or heaven,
There's not a task to mankind given,
There's not a blessing or a woe,
There's not a whispered "yes" or "no,"
There's not a life, or death, or birth
Without a woman in it.

C.E. BOWMAN

It's how a mother helps
her daughter leave the nest that
enables them both to fly high.

Use what talents you possess:
the woods would be very silent
if no birds sang there except those
who sang best.
HENRY VAN DYKE

The wise mother, training her daughter
not for the moment but for all time,
will realize that there are no small
things where a child is concerned;
that some things, apparently the most
trivial, will have far-reaching results.
MARY WOOD-ALLEN

In a Mom's Words

When my daughter was barely more than a toddler, we visited a Christmas theme park. While we were there, I ordered a special treat: funnel cake. Before I could tear off the first hunk of warm, powdered sugar-coated yumminess, my daughter pulled down the edge of my paper plate to take a look at what I was so excited about. Then she let it go. Powdered sugar flew like a holiday snowstorm, transforming my black outfit into something reminiscent of a Dalmatian. My daughter was horrified. She burst into tears—at the same time I burst out laughing.

This moment could have gone either way. I could've been angry or amused. I'm grateful laughter was my first inclination. But that hasn't always been the case. My daughter is grown now, but this memory still comes to mind every year around the holidays. It's a gift in it's own right, a reminder to not take the "small stuff" too seriously.

V.J.K.

There is nothing in the world
so irresistibly contagious as laughter
and good humor.

CHARLES DICKENS

Make it your habit to not be
critical about small things.

EDWARD EVERETT HALE

Life pays a bonus to those who learn
that laughter is a vital part of living.
It is one of God's richest gifts.

EDWIN DAVIS

My Friend–Inspiration

I was blessed to be chosen your mother,
Thrilled by your very first glance,
Awed by each new word and gesture,
Amazed by each step you would chance.

I was blessed to be chosen your mother,
To watch you become who you are—
So clever, so charming, so darling,
A scholar, a singer, a star.

I was blessed to be chosen your mother,
To be there for bad times and good.
To offer advice—sometimes wanted—
And often times just when I should.

I was blessed to be chosen your mother.
Now I watch as you're out on your own.
A Christian, my friend—inspiration.
A woman, a wonder, all grown.

KIM KNIGHT

NOTEWORTHY MOMS OF THE ANIMAL KINGDOM!

ELEPHANTS are pregnant for 22 months. The 250-pound baby Mom delivers is blind and totally dependent on her and the herd for survival. But Mom has a great circle of friends. Other elephants, called "allmothers" take over babysitting duty so Mom has time to eat, so she can continue to nurse her newborn.

ORANGUTAN newborns cling to their mom's stomach for the first four months of their lives, never letting go. They also breastfeed for five years. Maybe that's why orangutan moms only give birth about once every eight years. Orangutan sons leave Mom at an earlier age than do her daughters. They stick around longer to pick up tips on mothering.

POLAR BEAR moms sleep through the delivery of their babies. Lucky them! However their pregnancy and parent-hood isn't all fun and games. When first pregnant, moms eat enough to double their weight. Then they build a "mom cave" where they settle in for up to eight months, fasting the whole time. Cubs are born blind, weighing less than two pounds. While male polar bears have been known to eat cubs, Moms often adopt abandoned cubs, caring for them along with their own newborns for their first several years of life.

OCTOPUS moms have big families–laying 20,000 to 50,000 eggs. Mom "decorates" the nursery with her own children, using an elaborate system of dividing all of her eggs into groups. Mom spends the next few months pushing water currents around her eggs so they'll receive enough oxygen. Until Mom's eggs hatch, she's so busy defending her children from predators and working hard to circulate currents of water, that she isn't able to hunt. Often she will resort to (gulp!) eating her own arms for sustenance.

NEED A CHEERLEADER?

For a mother, there is something more painful than childbirth. It's seeing your child fail. Maybe you don't get the job you've been hanging your future on or the part you'd hoped for in the school play. It could be something as small as failing to fully cook your first Thanksgiving turkey or as big as ending your marriage. Regardless of what it is, when you hurt, we hurt.

But your lives are not ours. You have the freedom to make your own choices. Sometimes, as your mothers, we may believe those choices hinder you from reaching the amazing potential we see so clearly in you. At times like those, frankly, it's hard for us to keep our mouths shut. But we try. As for the other times, when disappointment or heartbreak seem to come out of nowhere, we hope you know how hard we're rooting for you. We've been your biggest fans since birth. Wherever life leads you, we'll be there by your side, ready to extend a hand, a tissue or a word of prayer.

Behold, I do not give lectures
or a little charity,
When I give, I give myself.
WALT WHITMAN

Love me when I least deserve it, because
that's when I really need it.
PROVERB

In a Mom's Words...

I gave birth to my two best friends! Other than being born on the same day, my darling twin daughters never did anything at the same time. They didn't sleep at the same time. They tag-teamed me on naps. When one was hungry the other wasn't. My girls didn't learn to crawl, walk, talk or read at the same time.

They never did anything together–until I had an instant empty nest when they left for college on the same day! Not only were the Twins leaving home, but being separated from each other for the first time. It was traumatic and exciting for all concerned. My girls are home for their senior year of college. My nest is temporarily full again, not with the cute little girls who grew up here, but with two beautiful, smart, funny, independent women! I know this time together is now the exception, not the rule. That makes me cherish this brief season all the more.

J.L.M.

*There are two things
in life for which we are
never truly prepared: Twins.*

JOSH BILLINGS

*The woman who creates
and sustains a home and under whose
hands children grow up to be strong
and pure men and women, is a creator
second only to God.*

HELEN HUNT JACKSON

*Even twins
are still one-of-a-kind.*

Noteworthy Moms and Daughters

Laura Ingalls Wilder is most widely recognized as the author of the *Little House on the Prairie* series, which was later turned into a popular television show. Inspired by her childhood memories of homesteading on farmland in Kansas, Laura's books might not have been published if it were not for the encouragement and tenacity of her daughter, Rose, who helped push for their publication after the Great Depression. Since 1931, this series has never gone out of print.

Rose Wilder Lane excelled in her own writing career as a journalist, travel writer, novelist and political theorist. She was also one of the founders of the American libertarian movement, along with Ayn Rand.

In the Words of
Laura Ingalls Wilder...

"Home is the nicest word there is."

"A good laugh overcomes more difficulties and dissipates more dark clouds than any other one thing."

"The real things haven't changed. It is still best to be honest and truthful; to make the most of what we have; to be happy with simple pleasures; and have courage when things go wrong."

"Remember well, and bear in mind, a constant friend is hard to find."

WHAT YOUR MOM REALLY WANTS FOR MOTHER'S DAY

- *For you to "friend" her on social media*
- *Clothes you've borrowed: returned*
- *Any money you promised you'd pay back*
- *A grandchild*
- *To hear your voice*
- *To hear an apology for the stretch marks you gave her*
- *To hear the words, "I love you" and "Thanks!"*
- *Your attention*
- *Your love*

*Only the heart knows how
to find what is precious.*
DOSTOYEVSKY

*We should all have at least one person
who loves us in spite of how we behave
today, one person who believes we're
not stuck where we are, but just passing
through to something better.*

Last night, my darling, as you slept,
*   I thought I heard you sigh;*
And to your little crib I crept,
*   And watched a space thereby;*
And then I stooped and kissed your brow,
*   For oh! I love you so—*
You are too young to know it now,
*   But some time you shall know!*

EUGENE FIELDS

Children grow up so quickly
and leave one, and I would long
that mine should take nothing but the
recollection of love and happiness from
their home with them into the world's
fight, knowing that they have there
always a safe harbor, and open arms
to comfort and encourage them
when they are in trouble.

PRINCESS ALICE MAUD MARY,
DAUGHTER OF QUEEN VICTORIA

Sweet is the smile of home;
the mutual look,
When hearts are of each other sure.

JOHN KEBLE

The amicable loosening of the bond between daughter and mother is one of the most difficult tasks of education.

ALICE BALINT-SZÉKELY-KOVÁCS

Nothing will draw a daughter home from college like a mother's love… or a bag of dirty laundry.

I write you letters by the thousands in my thoughts.

BEETHOVEN

THE RED SHOES

The day my daughter, my youngest, left for college left me feeling displaced. I was like a person who'd had the job of her dreams for almost twenty years and was suddenly laid off. I was fully aware she had her own life to live. Now I just had to figure out what I was going to do with mine.

Being a "touchstone" kind of person, I made a spur of the moment decision. After helping my daughter move into her college dorm, about 100 miles from our home, I stopped off at the mall. I'd always wanted a pair of red shoes, but felt they were too frivolous to spend my money on. But it was time to celebrate a season of new beginnings for both my daughter and me. My new red shoes helped me dance my way into the second act of my life with a lighter heart. They were a visible reminder that my coveted role of "mom" was ready to expand into the precious role of "friend."

V.J.K.

The Nest is Empty

The house is so quiet.
The dishes are clean.
The beds are all made
And there's time to daydream.

The car pools are finished
And chore charts are through.
Everything's perfect—
Except missing you.

Yet I know each prayer,
Each rule and each kiss,
Each heart-to-heart talk
Has helped lead us to this...

The day that my daughter
Leaves her childhood home
To stretch out her wings
And fly free on her own.

VICKI J. KUYPER

I'll always love you…